WORLD HERITAGE

Protecting Ancient Heritage

Brendan and Debbie Gallagher

Smart Apple Media
P.O. Box 3263
Mankato, MN, 56002

First published in 2010 by
MACMILLAN EDUCATION AUSTRALIA PTY LTD
15–19 Claremont St, South Yarra, Australia 3141

Visit our web site at www.macmillan.com.au or go directly to www.macmillanlibrary.com.au

Associated companies and representatives throughout the world.

Library of Congress Cataloging-in-Publication Data

Gallagher, Brendan.
    Protecting ancient heritage / Brendan and Debbie Gallagher.
        p. cm. — (World heritage)
    Includes index.
    ISBN 978-1-59920-577-9 (library bound)
    1. Historic sites—Conservation and restoration—Juvenile literature. 2. Antiquities—Collection and preservation—Juvenile literature. 3. Cultural property—Protection—Juvenile literature. 4. World Heritage areas—Juvenile literature. I. Gallagher, Debbie, 1969– II. Title.
    CC135.G347 2011
    930.1—dc22
                                2009053003

Publisher: Carmel Heron
Managing Editor: Vanessa Lanaway
Editor: Kirstie Innes-Will
Proofreader: Paige Amor
Designer: Kerri Wilson
Page layout: Kerri Wilson
Photo researcher: Legend Images
Illustrator: Guy Holt
Production Controller: Vanessa Johnson

Manufactured in China by Macmillan Production (Asia) Ltd.
Kwun Tong, Kowloon, Hong Kong
Supplier Code: CP December 2009

Acknowledgments

The author and the publisher are grateful to the following for permission to reproduce copyright material:

Cover photograph of Macchu Picchu © Jarnogz/Dreamstime.com

Photographs courtesy of:
Michael Amendolia with permission of the traditional owners, 31; Ashley Kalagian Blunt, 27; Cahokia Mounds State Historic Site/Michael Hampshire, 10, 11; © Nathan Benn/Corbis, 18; © Gianni Dagli Orti/Corbis, 8; © Robert Holmes/Corbis, 15; © Bugsy/Dreamstime.com, 23; © Jarnogz/Dreamstime.com, 1, 16; © Steba/Dreamstime.com, 24, 25; © Tudorish/Dreamstime.com, 22; ePublicist.ca 2006, 19; © Facundo/fotolia, 26; Eitan Abramovich/AFP/Getty Images, 17; © 2008 Jupiterimages Corporation, 9; Greg Elms/Lonely Planet Images, 7; Paolo Morandotti, 13; Kenneth Garrett/National Geographic Stock, 20; Martin Gray/National Geographic Stock, 21; O. Louis Mazzatenta/National Geographic Stock, 6; Photolibrary/Barbagallo Franco, 28; Photolibrary/JTB Photo, 12; Photolibrary/David Wall, 30; © Lakis Fourouklas/Shutterstock, 14; Wikimedia Commons photo by Artemio Urbina, 29.

While every care has been taken to trace and acknowledge copyright, the publisher tenders their apologies for any accidental infringement where copyright has proved untraceable. Where the attempt has been unsuccessful, the publisher welcomes information that would redress the situation.

Please note

Contents

When a word in the text is printed in **bold**, look for its meaning in the glossary boxes.

World Heritage

There are places around the world that are important to all peoples. We call these places the world's heritage. Some of these places are human creations, such as the pyramids of Egypt. Some are natural creations, such as the Great Barrier Reef of Australia.

The World Heritage List

The World Heritage List is a list of **sites** that must be protected because they have some kind of outstanding importance for the world. This list was created in 1972, and new places are added every year. Each site on the World Heritage List belongs to one of the following categories:

 NATURAL – for example, waterfalls, forests, or deserts

 CULTURAL – for example, a building or a site where an event occurred

 MIXED – if it has both natural and cultural features

UNESCO

UNESCO, the United Nations Educational, Scientific, and Cultural Organization, is the organization that maintains the World Heritage List. Find out more at www.unesco.org.

World Heritage Criteria

A place can be **inscribed** on the World Heritage List if it meets at least one of these ten **criteria**, and is an outstanding example of it. The criteria are:

 i a masterpiece of human creative genius

 ii a site representing the sharing of human ideas

 iii a site representing a special culture or civilization

 iv a historical building or landscape from a period of history

 v a site representing or important to a traditional culture

 vi a site representing an important event, idea, living tradition, or belief

 vii a very beautiful or unique natural site

 viii a site showing evidence of Earth's history

 ix an important ecosystem

 x an important natural habitat for species protection

KEY TERMS

sites	places
inscribed	added to
criteria	rules or requirements

Protecting Ancient Heritage

Protecting Ancient Heritage is about protecting places on Earth that are excellent examples of a past culture or **civilization**. Some of these cultures still exist today, but whether they continue in the present or not, protecting our ancient **heritage** is important to the entire world. We can learn about past civilizations from the ruins that they left behind. This study is called **archaeology**.

 ## Criteria for Protecting Ancient Heritage

Many of the places in this book are important for many reasons. This book focuses on just one reason: how a place shows us evidence of a special culture or civilization. This is reason iii on the list of criteria for being on the World Heritage List.

Protecting World Heritage

Governments around the world have all agreed to protect the sites on the World Heritage List. A site that is not being properly looked after may be put on the List of World Heritage in Danger. See http://whc.unesco.org/en/158/

This map shows the location of the World Heritage sites covered in this book.

civilization	the culture and society of a particular group in history
heritage	culture and traditions passed down through generations
archaeology	studying cultures from their remains

Archaeological Areas of Pompei, Herculaneum, and Torre Annunziata

The Archaeological Areas of Pompei, Herculaneum, and Torre Annunziata are the ruins of three ancient towns in Italy which were destroyed by a volcanic eruption. The areas were built by the Ancient Romans, who formed an enormous **empire** around the Mediterranean Sea.

FACT FILE

The ruins of Pompei, Herculaneum, and Torre Annunziata protect evidence of the Ancient Roman civilization.

Category:

Criteria:

Pompei was the largest town to be destroyed by the eruption of Mount Vesuvius.

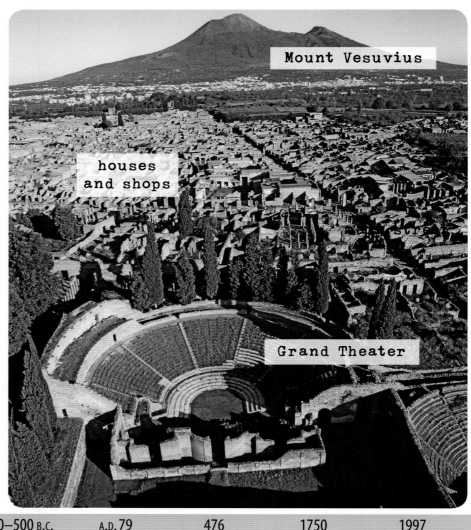

Mount Vesuvius

houses and shops

Grand Theater

TIMELINE

1000 B.C.	600–500 B.C.	A.D. 79	476	1750	1997
The Roman civilization begins in Italy.		Mount Vesuvius erupts.		People dig up the ruins of the towns.	
	Pompei is established.		The Roman civilization ends.		The site is inscribed on the World Heritage List.

Tourism brings money but also causes damage to Pompei.

Important Features

The eruption of Mount Vesuvius covered Herculaneum, a holiday resort for rich Romans, in 65 feet (20 meters) of **lava** and boiling mud. It also buried Pompei and Torre Annunziata in ashes and stones. These towns remained just as they were on the day the volcano erupted, until they were dug up. Houses and shops run along the paved streets, and you can still see the messages that the people of Pompei wrote on their walls.

> **Did You Know?**
> On one of the walls of Pompei, someone wrote: "Celadus the gladiator, idol of all the girls: three fights, three wins."

Issues

The ash and dust protected the ruins for hundreds of years. Once people dug out the towns, wind, rain, snow, and heat **eroded** the ruins. Scientists are working to control or prevent this. Future discoveries in the area may be kept buried in order to keep them safe.

GLOSSARY

empire	a group of nations and kingdoms with one ruler
lava	hot, melted rock
eroded	wore away

Archaeological Sites of Mycenae and Tiryns

The Archaeological Sites of Mycenae and Tiryns are the ruins of two different cities located on small hills in the south of Greece. These **citadels** were once the two greatest cities of the Mycenaean civilization. The Mycenaeans were an early Greek people.

FACT FILE

GREECE

The ruins of Mycenae and Tiryns protect evidence of the Mycenaean civilization.

Category:

Criteria:

Most of the ruins of Mycenae, such as this grave circle, date from the 1300s to 1200s B.C., when the Mycenaean civilization was at its height.

grave circle

walls

citadel

TIMELINE

1600 B.C.	1400–1200 B.C.	A.D. 1999
The Mycenaean civilization begins.	The Mycenaean civilization is at its peak.	The archaeological sites are inscribed on the World Heritage List.

Important Features

Mycenae and Tiryns, 12 miles (20 kilometers) apart, were surrounded by walls that were about 26 feet (8 meters) thick and at least 43 feet (13 m) in height. In later times, the walls were called cyclopean walls, because people believed they were built by mythical one-eyed giants called Cyclopses. Each city had a palace in the center. The floor of the palace at Tiryns is decorated with drawings of dolphins and octopuses.

Issues

Both Mycenae and Tiryns are managed very strictly. At both sites, ruins have been strengthened and restored. For example, part of the wall at Tiryns was in danger of collapsing, but restoration work has strengthed the walls. Mycenae is surrounded by farmland, and there are strict rules about what can be built around the ancient city.

Many gold items, such as this face mask, were discovered in the grave circle at Mycenae.

> ### Did You Know?
> The great Greek poet Homer mentions both Mycenae and Tiryns in his poetry.

GLOSSARY

citadels   fortresses in or near a city

Cahokia Mounds State Historic Site

Cahokia Mounds State Historic Site is an area containing 70 built mounds of earth, near the Mississippi River in the center of the United States. The area was one of the largest settlements in North America during the years A.D. 1050 to 1200.

slanted sides

staircase

Monks Mound once had wooden buildings on it and a wooden staircase where this concrete staircase is now.

TIMELINE

A.D. 700	1050	Around 1400	1966	1982
People begin to settle in the Cahokia area.	Mound building begins in the area.	The Mississippian civilization begins to decline.	Cahokia is listed as a historic place.	The site is inscribed on the World Heritage List.

This is an artist's impression of Cahokia at its peak, around A.D. 1100.

Important Features

Beginning around A.D. 500, a mound-building society began to develop in the area of the Mississippi River. This society was made up of many different Native American peoples, speaking different languages. This civilization is now called Mississippian. Many of the mounds they built had pyramid-shaped bases. The tops were flattened and houses and other buildings were built on them. Up to 20,000 Mississippians lived in the area.

Issues

There are plans to build a **landfill** site within 2,300 feet (700 meters) of the Cahokia Mounds site. There is already a landfill site visible from the top of Monks Mound, and many people do not want a second site to be built. However, other people argue that the landfill site would not affect the World Heritage area.

Did You Know?

Monks Mound is the largest of the Cahokia mounds. Its base is 1,000 feet (305 m) by 700 feet (213 m), making it larger than the base of Egypt's largest pyramid, the Pyramid of Khufu.

GLOSSARY

landfill   garbage buried in the ground

Capital Cities and Tombs of the Ancient Koguryo Kingdom

FACT FILE

CHINA

The Capital Cities and Tombs of the Ancient Koguryo Kingdom protect evidence of the Koguryo empire.

Category: ✋

Criteria:

The Capital Cities and Tombs of the Ancient Koguryo Kingdom are the ruins of three ancient cities in northeast China. The Koguryo Kingdom emerged in the area in the first century B.C., and soon came to rule parts of northern China and Korea.

General's Tomb

entrance

The General's Tomb is believed to be the burial place of the twentieth king of the Koguryo Kingdom.

TIMELINE

37 B.C.	7 B.C.	A.D. 209	427	668	2004
The Koguryo Kingdom begins with the building of its first capital city.	Guonei City becomes the capital of the Koguryo Kingdom.	Wandu Mountain City is built.	Pyongyang, in modern North Korea, becomes the capital.	The Koguryo Kingdom falls to neighboring kingdoms after long wars.	The site is inscribed on the World Heritage List.

12

These tombs of Wandu Mountain City were built within the city's walls. The insides of many are decorated with images of fairies, dragons, and scenes from daily life.

Important Features

The three cities of the Koguryo were Wunu Mountain City, Guonei City, and Wandu Mountain City. These cities were built in harmony with their natural surroundings. Today, the site is centered around the modern cities of Ji'an and Huanren. It contains 14 **imperial** tombs, built of stones and holding members of the royal families. There are also 27 tombs of nobles.

Issues

Ancient Guonei City is located within the modern city of Ji'an. No new buildings are allowed to be built in the area. Buildings that were put up before the site was added to the World Heritage List will be removed. This will restore the area to how it looked in ancient times.

Did You Know?
The main weapon of the Koguryo people was the bow and arrow.

GLOSSARY

empire	a group of nations and kingdoms with one ruler
imperial	relating to an empire

Great Zimbabwe National Monument

The Great Zimbabwe National Monument is an area of stone-block ruins in Zimbabwe. From the A.D. 1000s to the 1400s, it was a city of more than 10,000 people. The people of Great Zimbabwe became rich through trading gold with their neighbors. They are the **ancestors** of the Shona people who still live in parts of Zimbabwe.

The Great Enclosure was the largest structure south of the Sahara Desert when it was built.

ruins of the Great Enclosure

valley ruins

TIMELINE

1000s
The building of Great Zimbabwe begins.

1450
The people abandon the settlement and migrate north.

1986
The Great Zimbabwe National Monument is inscribed on the World Heritage List.

The walls of the Great Enclosure are nearly 33 feet (10 meters) tall.

Important Features

The ruins include three areas – the hill fort, the valley ruins, and the Great Enclosure. The ruins of the valley were once the homes of the people, while the Great Enclosure was the home of the king. It is thought that the area was abandoned because the population became too large and could not find and grow enough food in the area.

Did You Know?

The word *Zimbabwe* means "stone houses." Zimbabwe gets its name from the stone houses in the area of the Great Zimbabwe National Monument.

Issues

Zimbabwe is a nation in political turmoil and it does not have enough money to support its people. This means that protecting places like the Great Zimbabwe National Monument is very difficult. Some of the walls of the ancient buildings have fallen over or are in danger of collapsing.

GLOSSARY

ancestors   people who came before you in your family

Historic Sanctuary of Machu Picchu

The Historic Sanctuary of Machu Picchu is an area of ruins high in the Andes mountains of Peru. A village was built there by the **emperor** of the Inca people, Pachacuteq, in the A.D. 1400s. The Incan civilization emerged in the A.D. 1200s and by A.D. 1500 most of the west coast of South America was part of their **empire**.

Wayna Picchu rises over Machu Picchu. It is 8,924 feet (2,720 meters) high.

Wayna Picchu peak

Temple of the Sun

houses

terraces

TIMELINE

A.D. 1438	1460	Around 1570	1981	1983
Pachacuteq comes to power.	The building of Machu Picchu begins.	The Spanish conquer the Incan Empire.	Machu Picchu is made a historical sanctuary.	The site is inscribed on the World Heritage List.

16

Care has to be taken to stop tourists damaging the Machu Picchu site.

Important Features

Pachacuteq built Machu Picchu as a place where he could relax and hunt. There were about 150 houses in the mountain village, as well as baths, temples, and palaces. The Incas built the houses from carefully cut blocks of stone that fitted together perfectly. The roofs were made from plant materials. The Incas also cut into the side of the mountain, creating **terraces** where they could grow crops.

Issues

Already, about 2,500 people visit Machu Picchu every day, but a new bridge below Machu Picchu could allow double that number to access the site. **Archaeologists** are worried that too many people visiting the site will damage it.

Did You Know?

Spanish soldiers first came into contact with the Incas in 1528, and within 50 years they had destroyed the civilization through war and disease.

GLOSSARY

emperor	the ruler of an empire
empire	a group of nations and kingdoms with one ruler
terraces	flat, raised banks with vertical or sloping sides
archeologists	people that study the remains of civilizations

Masada

Masada is a rocky mountain **plateau** overlooking the Dead Sea in Israel. The king of Judea, Herod the Great, turned the hill into a **fortified palace**. When the Jewish peoples of Judea fought with the Ancient Romans, Masada was the last place to be captured.

Masada stands between 328 and 1,312 feet (100 and 400 meters) above the surrounding area. It was very hard to attack.

FACT FILE

ISRAEL
ASIA
AFRICA

Masada protects evidence of the kingdom of Judea.

Category: ✋

Criteria: ⛰ 🏛 🌍

surrounding desert

western palace

plateau

synagogue

walls

northern palace on three levels

TIMELINE

37–4 B.C.	A.D. 66	70	73	2000
Herod the Great builds palaces and walls at Masada.	War breaks out between the Jewish peoples and the Romans.	The Romans take over Jerusalem and many people flee to Masada.	The Romans take over Masada.	Masada is inscribed on the World Heritage List.

18

Important Features

Herod the Great built three palaces at Masada. He also built bath houses and other buildings with mosaic floors, using Roman styles. Herod surrounded the hill with a strong wall, nearly 4,265 feet (1,300 meters) long, with 27 towers. After A.D. 66, the Jews built a **synagogue** at Masada.

Issues

Masada is in a remote desert, so human activities have not had a negative impact on it. Many of the buildings have been carefully restored. However, some people argue that the cable car that runs up the side of Masada spoils the ancient site, while others argue that it is needed to help people who could not climb the difficult path up the hill.

The remains of the synagogue at Masada can still be seen.

GLOSSARY

plateau	a wide, flat area in a high place
fortified palace	a palace surrounded with walls and other defences to protect it
synagogue	a Jewish place of worship

Memphis and its Necropolis — the Pyramid Fields from Giza to Dahshur

The Pyramid Fields protect evidence of the Ancient Egyptian civilization.

Category:

Criteria:

Memphis and its **Necropolis** – the Pyramid Fields from Giza to Dahshur is a combination of areas, containing ancient rock tombs, temples, and pyramids, in Egypt. The area was the capital city of Egypt from about 2700 to 2150 B.C. and the **pharaohs** were all crowned there.

The three main pyramids, Khufu, Khafre, and Memkaure, are very close to Cairo.

TIMELINE

2700–2200 B.C.	2575–2465	A.D. 1979
Memphis is the capital of the Old Kingdom of Egypt.	The pyramids and Great **Sphinx** are built at Memphis.	The site is inscribed on the World Heritage List.

The pyramids are now surrounded on three sides by the city of Cairo and pollution is damaging them.

Important Features

The pyramids are the tombs of pharaohs. Khufu is the largest of the pyramids and is often called the Great Pyramid of Giza. It was probably built by the pharaoh Khufu. To the east of Khufu is the Great Sphinx, a lion with the head of the pharaoh Khafre.

Issues

The pyramids of Giza are on the edge of the largest city in Egypt, Cairo. The city is continuing to grow and pollution is damaging the pyramids. Waste water has seeped into the earth, threatening the stability of the pyramids and especially of the Sphinx, but **archaeologists** have installed pumps to remove the water every day.

Did You Know?

In ancient times the pyramid of Khufu was listed as one of the Seven Wonders of the World.

GLOSSARY

necropolis	a cemetery or burial ground
pharaohs	kings and queens of Egypt
sphinx	a mythical creature with the body of a lion and the head of a man, ram, or hawk
archeologists	people that study the remains of civilizations

Mesa Verde National Park

Mesa Verde National Park is a semi-dry **plateau** in Colorado. The plateau is cut through by **canyons**, containing more than 600 homes and buildings built into the cliffs. The homes were built by the Ancestral Pueblo people, **ancestors** of today's Pueblo people.

FACT FILE

UNITED STATES

Mesa Verde National Park protects evidence of the Ancestral Pueblo civilization.

Category:

Criteria:

The building known as Cliff Palace had more than 181 rooms.

plateau

canyon face

alcove

Cliff Palace

TIMELINE

600	1300s	1906	1978
The Ancestral Pueblo people begin to settle in the Mesa Verde area.	The Ancestral Pueblo people abandon their settlement.	Mesa Verde is made a national park to protect its unique buildings.	The site is inscribed on the World Heritage List.

Important Features

The plateau of the Mesa Verde National Park is 8,530 feet (2,600 meters) above sea level. Water has caused **erosion** over thousands of years, forming **alcoves** in the base of the canyon walls. While the Ancestral Pueblo people actually spent more of their time living on the plateau, they are best remembered for the buildings they created in these canyon alcoves. In the 1300s, they abandoned the Mesa Verde area for unknown reasons and migrated south to New Mexico and Texas.

Issues

The erosion that created the alcoves continues today and can damage the walls and foundations of many of the Mesa Verde buildings. **Archaeologists** keep an eye on these processes and reduce or reverse any damage that may occur.

Archaeologists look after the buildings to prevent further damage from erosion.

GLOSSARY

plateau	a wide, flat area in a high place
canyons	deep valleys with steep sides
ancestors	people who came before you in your family
erosion	the process of being worn away
alcoves	indents or very shallow caves
archeologists	people that study the remains of civilizations

Persepolis

Persepolis was the ancient capital of the Achaemenid Persian **Empire**. Persia is an old name for Iran and the Achaemenid Empire was the largest empire in the ancient world. It stretched from India to Egypt and Greece. The Achaemenid Empire came to its end in 330 B.C. when Alexander the Great of Greece **looted** and destroyed Persepolis.

The architecture of Persepolis is Persian but it was also influenced by Egyptian, Greek, Assyrian, and Babylonian styles. The Persians had a huge empire so they drew on other cultures they conquered.

FACT FILE

ASIA

IRAN

Persepolis protects evidence of the Achaemenid Persian Empire.

Category: ✋

Criteria: 🧎 🔺 🌍

palaces

Hall of 100 Columns

reliefs

TIMELINE

518 B.C.
Darius I builds palaces at Persepolis and makes it his capital.

330 B.C.
Persepolis is looted and burned by Alexander the Great.

A.D. 1979
Persepolis is inscribed on the World Heritage List.

This relief from the Palace of Darius shows Persian warriors.

Important Features

The center of Persepolis was on a stone **terrace**, half natural and half built. It was a city only for the royal family. The city ruins include palaces and great halls, such as the Hall of 100 Columns, where the kings held important events. The walls of the hall are decorated with **reliefs**. The palaces were reached by massive staircases. The sides of the staircases are also decorated with reliefs.

Issues

The main problems facing Persepolis come from farms and factories moving ever closer to the borders of the World Heritage site. Farming and industry can cause air pollution. The managers of Persepolis are trying to measure the pollution and find out what impact it is having on the buildings and reliefs.

Did You Know?

The Roman historian Plutarch wrote that when Alexander the Great looted the treasures of Persepolis, he took them away on 20,000 mules and 5,000 camels.

GLOSSARY

empire	a group of nations and kingdoms with one ruler
looted	took everything of value from
terrace	a flat, raised bank with vertical or sloping sides
reliefs	sculptures carved on walls

Pre-Hispanic City of Teotihuacan

The **Pre-Hispanic** City of Teotihuacan is an area of pyramids, palaces, temples, and brilliant artwork in central Mexico. Teotihuacan was the first great city of the Americas but it was abandoned in the A.D. 600s. The identity of the people of Teotihuacan is not known.

FACT FILE

MEXICO

The Pre-Hispanic City of Teotihuacan protects the remains of a lost civilization.

Category:

Criteria:

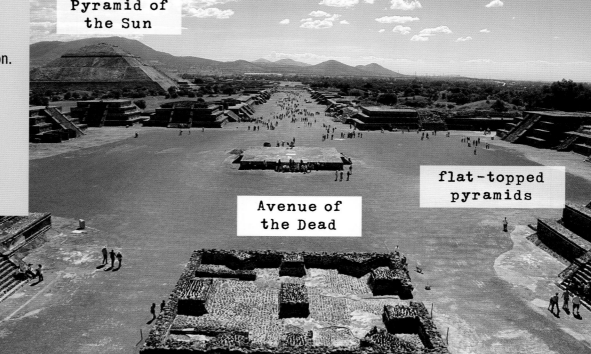

Pyramid of the Sun

Avenue of the Dead

flat-topped pyramids

Teotihuacan was one of the largest cities in the world at its time.

TIMELINE

200 B.C.
People begin to settle in the Teotihuacan area.

A.D. 300–600
The city of Teotihuacan has a population of at least 125,000 people.

650
The Teotihuacan civilization collapses.

1987
The site is inscribed on the World Heritage List.

Important Features

The people who built Teotihuacan planned their city very carefully. The Avenue of the Dead runs through the middle of the city. It begins at the Pyramid of the Moon, passes the 246-foot (75-meter) high Pyramid of the Sun and continues as far as the Ciudadela. Ciudadela is the Spanish word for **citadel**. The city was abandoned after a great fire. The fire may have been lit by an invading army but it is more likely that the people of Teotihuacan started it in a rebellion against their leaders.

Did You Know?

When the Aztecs came across the abandoned city, many centuries later, they called it "the place where the gods were created."

The sound and light fittings have damaged the surface of the Temple of the Sun pyramid.

Issues

In 2008, the local government installed a sound and light show to entertain tourists during the evenings. The light fittings bolted onto the sides of the pyramids have damaged the pyramids. In 2009 the Mexican government temporarily stopped the sound and light project.

GLOSSARY

pre-Hispanic	from the time before the Spanish conquered South and Central America in the 1500s
citadel	a fortress in or near a city

Rapa Nui National Park

Rapa Nui National Park is an archaeological area containing houses, ceremonial structures, wall paintings, and up to 900 large stone statues on Easter Island. The statues, called moai, were built by the Rapanui. They were a Polynesian people who settled on the islands some time after A.D 300. and lived there in complete isolation for hundreds of years.

FACT FILE

Rapa Nui National Park protects evidence of the Rapanui civilization.

Category:

Criteria:

moai

platform

These moai on Easter Island have been restored as evidence of the Rapanui civilization.

TIMELINE

300–1200	1250–1500	1722	1888	1935	1995
The Rapanui arrive at Easter Island at some point during this period.	The Rapanui carve the moai.	Dutch explorers find Rapa Nui on Easter Sunday and call it Easter Island.	Easter Island becomes part of Chile.	Easter Island is made a national park.	The site is inscribed on the World Heritage List.

Some statues appear to be only heads, but the body is buried below the ground.

Important Features

The Rapanui cut blocks of stone from the inside of one of the island's **extinct** volcanoes. They then moved the statues to platforms and placed them facing toward the center of the island. The Rapanui believed the statues, which were between 6.5 and 65 feet (2 and 20 meters) in height, were their **ancestors**, protecting them and their land.

Issues

Many of the statues have fallen over. While some experts would like to restore the statues, many local people prefer that the statues remain as they are. They believe that there are enough statues already standing and claim that statues that have been restored are deteriorating quicker than the ones still on the ground.

GLOSSARY

extinct	dead or no longer active
ancestors	people who came before you in your family

Willandra Lakes Region

Willandra Lakes Region is a desert landscape of 18 dried lakes in Australia. On the eastern sides of the lakes, there are crescent-shaped dunes of sand and clay, called *lunettes*. Within the lunettes, there are the ancient remains of a people who once lived in the area.

FACT FILE

AUSTRALIA

The Willandra Lakes Region protects evidence of one of the oldest civilizations on Earth.

Category:

Criteria:

These formations at the Willandra Lakes are called the Walls of China.

desert landscape

lunettes

dry lake bed

TIMELINE

45,000 years ago	40,000 years ago	1968	1974	1979	1981
Humans live around the Willandra Lakes.	Mungo Woman and Mungo Man are buried.	The remains of Mungo Woman are discovered.	The remains of Mungo Man are discovered.	The heart of the Willandra Lakes region is made a national park.	The site is inscribed on the World Heritage List.

Important Features

It was once thought that **Indigenous Australian peoples** first lived in Australia 8,000 years ago, but then two separate burials of Indigenous Australians – called Mungo Man and Mungo Woman – were discovered at Willandra Lakes. They showed that people lived in the area about 40,000 years ago. The body of Mungo Woman is evidence of the oldest **cremation** on Earth. When they lived there, the lakes were filled with water and a **rain forest** covered the landscape. Indigenous Australians lived beside the lakes.

Issues

The most popular part of Willandra Lakes is Lake Mungo and its lunette. Visitors walking on the dune can damage it, so the park managers have built boardwalks over it. There are plans to build more boardwalks.

Did You Know?

In 2003, about 460 footprints were discovered at Lake Mungo, dating back about 20,000 years.

Elders of the three traditional Indigenous groups of the Willandra Lakes area look at the ancient footprints found at Lake Mungo.

GLOSSARY

Indigenous Australian peoples	the first people to live in Australia
cremation	the act of burning bodies
rain forest	a forest that gets a lot of rain

Index